Sailing the Air

George Marsh

Salting the Air

Printed in a limited edition of 200 copies
of which this is number 67 /200

For the Venerable Myokyo-ni, in gratitude for her teaching.

Salting the Air

George Marsh

Waning Moon Press

Some of these haiku have been published in *Blithe Spirit, Bare Bones, Haiku Spirit, Haiku Quarterly, Presence* and *The Haiku Attic.* Waning Moon extends thanks to the editors of these journals.

Also available from Waning Moon Press in this series:

Echoes in the Heart by Michael Gunton

The Earth Drawn Inwards by Cicely Hill

My Green Wife: Koji, Stefanov and Other Poets
translated by Chiyoko Mukai, Mitko Vassilev and George Marsh

Words on the Wind by James Norton

SUPPORTED BY
THE NATIONAL LOTTERY
THROUGH
THE **ARTS COUNCIL**
OF ENGLAND

Cover:

Drawing by Murakami Iwao

Typography and book design:

Ian Noble

British Library Cataloguing in Publication Data.

A catalogue record for this book is available from the British Library.

ISBN: 0-9529775-2-4

Waning Moon Press

10 Gains Road, Southsea, Portsmouth PO4 OPL UK

Telephone & Facsimile 01705 793935

International +44 1705 793935

How do you know but ev'ry Bird that cuts the airy way,
Is an immense world of delight, clos'd by your senses five?

William Blake *The Marriage of Heaven and Hell*

in the time it takes
to make toast and coffee
stars fade

coming from her house
he stops to stroke
the cherry blossom

everybody smiles at me today -
my silly new shirt

a rare man
hear him pissing noisily
in the centre

posing for the camera flash
when the door creaks open
and a shy face appears

gnarled love-signs
cut through the bark
in the year of my birth

down on my knees
hands full of mud
when spring comes

in the gutter
blossom rises
on the flood

held still
in the blur of wingbeats
the kestrel's eye

fearsome Hell's Angel
revving at the crossing
waiting for a child

we're watching birds
when the cat breaks off
to suck its toe

deep in the foliage
a feathering -
trembling red berries

in the Rose Garden
a man I don't much like
enjoying the sun

a swarm of dunlin roves
stabbing the mud - but Monsieur
Curlew strolls and probes

what do you know
bald pinhead dandelion?
she loves me not!

heat haze and shaking
in the red tree
a trapped breeze

bread and water
with goat's cheese
and a tomato!

the massive copper beech
is never so still
as in this drizzle

a discharge
oozes from the bull's eye -
how hard his cheek!

beetle scratching
on the wind
fairground music

missed it   the moment to join in the laugh

a moorhen, a lapwing
and a limping gull
share the champagne mud

skimming the glare
a cormorant claps
its shadow's wingtips

shadow of my head -
outline of nothing
on the bright ripples

the bullock's eye glitters -
from deep in his belly
opens a MU

I've fetched up here
where my son makes fun of me
and birds sing

a glittering pellet
of blue beetle husks
found on the hilltop

walking in cloud
hearing my son
explain something

after a day
deep in the hills
the sound of traffic

the taste of tea -
shadows gather in the room
before dusk comes

the gull soars on nothing
but slight corrections
to the tilt of its nose

Evening at Chithurst

evening at Chithurst -
there is nothing in the world
but the blackbird's song

the song notes
stitch me
to earth and to clouds

each white head of cloud
takes in
distinct whistled trills

hands cupping water
in the stream - the blackbird's
voice flows

air of the shrine-room
salted with song - each
meditator breathing

airhead?
who would be anything else
when the blackbird sings

in the silence
between bursts of song
come bursts of heart

eager-eye
whatever you are singing
I agree

Two Sonnets

Teal

You won't understand but you are you are
beautiful - conker headsheen, brilliant green
cheeksplash - you scoot about, you roundbeamed tar,
pushing up a chill breastwave, silver ermine
wings wrapped to the gunwales where a strake
of pale fungus brown runs to your glistening
caramel transom. Circumnavi-drake
beached in the shallows now and listing
you suckseed shlurp the slime fringe line for what
your blood needs your genes crave the winter Tao
ignites below to glimmer in your gut.
You're a hot greed, a cold eye, swimming now -
no Romance clogs your head, nothing ideal;
you glide without the ache of thought, male teal.

High Force

Rising through the rustle of wind in dry leaves
a thrum. Approach, and roar fills the woods:
the sound of the red river powdering. Each drop
turning white in the interminable air,
suffers a loss in which it is alone, feels
vivid, finds, falling through dry nothing
what being liquid was. What rock gives
is to receive. The drops soften, foam into fissures,
press through pores in the flooded basalt.
Down at the pool's edge in the pebbled shallows,
the sound of the red river mending:
water-stories eddy, purling away by tone,
like our conversation, the roar of all that
screaming in emptiness, beating on stone.

Langstone Harbour

On 7th. November 1991 my father died. I walked by the shores of Langstone Harbour.

> winter wind -
> two geese turn
> a broad descending circle
> and end
> facing it
> knowing how to touch down
> lightly

At the wake my sons looked after me sweetly, talked of family memories and had me laughing. I returned to Langstone Harbour and watched yachts on their moorings as fishing boats motored by.

> I lift, judder
> spin and settle
> in your wake

water in the bay
no trace
of the splashy wingbeats

lowtide mudflats -
I breathe out
tremble

dense cloud
the colour of ashes
the sky is my father

Out walking one moonless midnight on Farlington Marshes, a bird sanctuary, I looked across the harbour to the city:

seen fom this dark place
over the waves - the lights
of the people sanctuary

And another night, fascinated by the waves, slopping inside a wreck with the life-force of the ocean:

between the ribs
of the broken boat
rises the moonlit tide

In the New Year:

bright cold morning -
for breakfast let's open
the last of his marmalade!

On the anniversary of his death I stand on the ferry pontoon at Eastney Point, tasting the windblown spray:

grief, and breathing
the salty fragrance
of the deep tide drift

More walking is good - by the Harbour, in the woods, and on the Heath by the family home:

minded by squirrels
the hawthorn and oak
and in the leafmould your ashes

under my foot
at every step
my father's ashes

Sesshin in May

monastery bells -
the incense the candles
the woodblocks the gong

light like mist
on the quarrytile floor
where a lacewing grooms

from far below, the rise in pitch
of a big kettle filling -
and in the stillness, a tickle

as into my ear creeps a guest
some little thing with a tread
as delicate as bliss

(A sesshin is a meditation retreat)

baby's in bed -
from the darkening mist
the cry of a swift

under the hill
tarmac whispers
echoes of passing

tinged with red
crescent moons
in the wake of the teal

in the dark
sitting with my rubber plant
listening to rain

behind the clouds
I can almost feel
the promised meteors

under a tree
the drunk stands
watching rain

stars
just out of reach
a cricket croaking

deep in the heart
of the darkening woods
the water's white roar

on a rusty buoy
the fog bell feels
each melancholy wave

phosphorescence at the oarblades -
from dark marshes
the gurgling of geese

stars fill the hatchway
swaying
to the smell of melon

sound of dance-music -
the last fishing boat
throbs into place

galaxies tremble
as a whirligig beetle
scoots the midnight pond

summer night
a duck glides
between moons

city night -
the restless roar of tyres
and a faint lone bell

vibrating
engines power us
from mist to mist

the bitter waves
cappuccinoed
in our wake

in the light of a crescent moon
pale leaves of willow

waking from storms -
sparrowcheeping
in a blue stillness

misty dawn -
under a waning moon
a sapling

pintglass brimming
he steps precisely
into the glare

summer's end nears -
now the slow bee allows
stroking of fur

blackeyed geese
with a sound like sorting banknotes
sieve the ripples

flying through
the pigeon's mind
the steelgrey sky

autumn dusk
and the river flows fast -
my aching knees

the Sage on the Inferior Man:
I nod and nod till I read
"...he nods."

stings my eyes
Remembrance Garden smoke
from the bonfire of leaves

the storm as a guest -
hailstones puddling
the dining-room carpet

a Pompey musher
strutting the gale
laughs at a tree's wild swirl

(A Pompey musher is a young man from Portsmouth, in the local dialect. Musher is derived from the Romany word *moosh*, for man. A Pompey musher has a macho swagger and plenty of attitude.)

she cried at a song,
some love song, gulping
the cold night air

in the winter wind
between derelict factories
waterripples

withered rosehips;
two coots and a fisherman
under thin willows

the sea-angler's girl
spends Christmas Eve
shrunk in a windbreak

late December -
sparrows splash and scream
in an angel's wing

New Year's Day -
outside, a magpie
inside, a ladybird

such a pleasure
saying please and thankyou
in spring sunshine

a hedgehog sound -
the brickie shuffling
his shovel in sand

words
you go to sleep now
I’ll stay out here